Rihanna
ANNUAL 2013

POSY EDWARDS

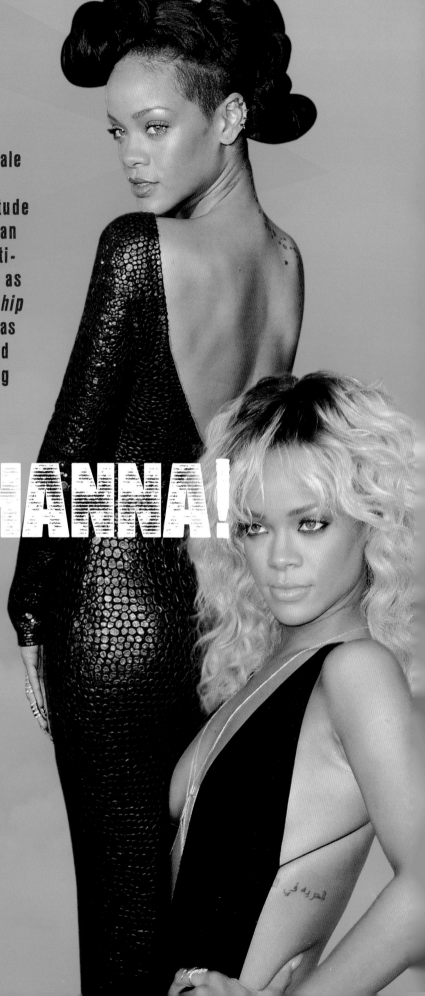

She`s one of the biggest-selling female artists in the world, known for her stunning voice, tough but sexy attitude and amazing looks. Rihanna is truly an international megastar — and a multi-talented one, too! She`s best known as a singer, but with the movie *Battleship* she`s making her name as an actress as well. And don`t forget she`s designed clothes for Armani! Is there anything this amazing woman can`t do?

MEET RIHANNA!

She`s made headlines for her personal life but shown that she can be strong, successful and sassy while becoming one of the biggest stars on the planet. Way to go Ri-Ri!

QUICK FACTS

NAME: Robyn Rihanna Fenty

NICKNAME: Ri-Ri

BORN: 20 February 1988 in Barbados

HEIGHT: 5' 8"

STAR SIGN: Pisces

SCHOOL: Combermere High School, Barbados

PARENTS: Monica and Ronald

SIBLINGS: Brothers Rajad and Rorrey

FAVOURITE BODY PART: Her bottom!

RIHANNA REVEALED

If she hadn't been a singer, Rihanna would have liked to be a TV host like Jerry Springer!

BECOMING RIHANNA

Nestled in the Atlantic Ocean near the Caribbean is the beautiful island of Barbados, and it was there that Robyn Rihanna Fenty was born on 20th February 1988. Her mum, Monica, was originally from the South American country of Guyana, while her dad Ronald is Bajan. Her mum worked as an accountant while her dad worked in a warehouse as a supervisor, and after Rihanna was born they had two more children, sons Rorrey (who's now 22) and Rajad (who's 16).
The family lived in a three-bedroom green and white bungalow in Bridgetown, and when she was old enough Rihanna would help her dad sell hats, belts and scarves from a stall on the street to earn extra money.

Growing up, Rihanna listened to music from an early age, especially reggae, and she was encouraged by her grandmother Carla to sing along. 'The neighbours used to complain a lot about how loud I was singing, but I didn't care,' she remembers. 'I had big dreams!' She used to sing Whitney Houston songs and the Disney tune 'A Whole New World' into her hairbrush, pretending she was on stage, and her neighbours – when they weren't telling her to be quiet – nicknamed her Robyn Redbreast because she sang so much.

FROM TOMBOY TO BEAUTY QUEEN

Although Rihanna used to sing all the time, she wasn't famous in Barbados: 'I used to sing at home, in the shower and in front of the mirror, but I wasn't a known singer in Barbados. I did one talent show at my high school, and I won it singing Mariah Carey's "Hero".'

She even tried her hand at other things – including entering beauty pageants as a teenager. Despite being a tomboy more interested in hanging out with her fellow cadets (the Bajan version of scouts, and Ri-Ri worked so hard at being a cadet she became a corporal), she put on make-up and styled her hair and then won a beauty contest when she was 15. 'I kind of laughed at these stupid pageants,' she remembers. 'But my friends at school dared me to do it, and my military training came in handy for learning to balance books on my head for the catwalk!'

It's no surprise to us that Rihanna won the competition, but she was shocked to get the prize, as she didn't even think she was beautiful. 'I only started wearing make-up after I won a school pageant. It was very new and weird to me. I was a barefoot tomboy and only in high school I started getting fussy with myself. That's when I started being very aware of what I looked like'.

When she wasn't singing or appearing in pageants, Rihanna spent her spare time at the beach, hanging with her best friend Shakira who lived across the street, or studying at school (her favourite subjects were Maths and Chemistry, and she hated P.E.). She also spent a lot of time with her dad, and he taught her to fish, swim and ride a bike and, she says, 'he's the one who made me tough and prepared me for the world.'

BOYS, BOYS, BOYS!

He didn't prepare her for the attention of boys though, and Rihanna didn't have her first kiss until she was a teenager. 'My first kiss was in high school, and it was the worst thing ever,' she told Rolling Stone magazine. 'I didn't kiss for, like, ever!' Instead of spending time with boys, Ri-Ri preferred to go out dancing with her girlfriends, which turned out to be good practice for a life on stage.

At home, as Rihanna approached the age of 16, things weren't going so well. There were difficulties at home, and in the end her mum and dad decided to separate and her dad moved out. To distract her from the troubles at home, Ri-Ri and her pals formed a girl group and the three of them would spend weekends practicing their songs and dance moves. All the dancing and singing practice came in handy a few months later when she met the man who would change her life…

RIHANNA REVEALED

'We basically spent the entire day on the beach with summer all year round… That was just normal for Barbados, but after I moved to America and I experienced all these different seasons – you don't get to see the ocean, where it's clear or it's baby blue. Whenever I've gone back to Barbados, I've really appreciated that a lot.'

Rihanna knew she was destined for stardom from a young age. And in the summer of 2003, Ri-Ri was introduced to a man named Evan Rogers, who was on holiday in Barbados with his wife. Rogers, along with his business partner Carl Sturken, wrote songs and produced music for artists including Christina Aguilera, Boyzone, Jessica Simpson, Mandy Moore and Kelly Clarkson. He met Rihanna – dressed in pink Capri trousers, a pink blouse and pink sneakers – and the two friends that made up the girl group she was in, but Rogers remembers that the moment Ri-Ri started to sing, he forgot there were two other girls in the room. 'She carried herself like a star even when she was 15. But the killer was when she opened her mouth to sing (Destiny's Child's cover of 'Emotion'). She was a little rough around the edges, but she had this edge to her voice.'

RIHANNA REVEALED

'I always knew I was gonna do this. I would say, "When I become a singer..." I knew I was gonna be somebody one day. Really and truly.'

DESTINED FOR GREATNESS

Evan Rogers offered to help Rihanna get a record deal. For the next year, she and her mum travelled between Barbados and Rogers' home in Stamford, Connecticut where he helped her polish her talent and get ready to record a demo tape that he could take to record companies. In the meantime, Rihanna signed to Rogers and Carl Sturken's production company, Syndicated Rhythm Productions, where she was given her own manager! They then made a demo tape of Ri-Ri singing in New York and it wasn't long before Def Jam, run by hip-hop star Jay-Z, called Rogers and asked to see Rihanna in person!

JAY-Z

RIHANNA REVEALED

'I'm super inspired by reggae music and it has been a part of me since I was born, and I grew up listening to it.'

'And that's when I really got nervous,' Rihanna remembers. 'I was like: "Oh God, he's right there, I can't look, I can't look, I can't look!" I remember being extremely quiet. I was very shy. I was cold the entire time. I had butterflies. I'm sitting across from Jay-Z. Like, Jay-Z. I was star-struck.' She sang Whitney's 'For the Love of Me', 'Pon de Replay' and a song Evan Rogers and Carl Sturken had written called 'The Last Time'.

'The audition definitely went well,' she says. 'They (Def Jam) locked me into the office till 3am. And Jay-Z said, "There's only two ways out. Out the door after you sign this deal. Or through this window..." And we were on the 29th floor. Very flattering.'

He was only joking, of course! In fact, he signed her on the spot to a six-album deal in February 2005, and Rihanna cancelled all the other meetings with record labels she had in her diary. She moved from her childhood home in Barbados to New York, where she stayed with Evan Rogers and his wife, and plans were put in place for her to record her first album, *Music of the Sun.*

MUSIC OF THE SUN

Plans were set in motion for Rihanna's debut album to be released in August 2005, so she went straight into the recording studio with Evan Rogers and Carl Sturken to work on one of the songs that would end up being the first single, 'Pon de Replay'. To begin with, she wasn't sure it was the song for her. 'When I first heard that song, I didn't want to do it, because it was very sing-songy and very… nursery-rhymish. But after I started recording it, I went along with it and started liking it. And people loved it!'

The album featured lots of the sounds Rihanna liked and grew up with – Caribbean music including reggae and soca (a style of calypso music), dance, pop and R&B. But the singer is quick to point out that her music is original too: 'My sound is really a fusion of reggae, hip-hop and R&B, with a little something different thrown in.'

Rihanna got to work with a host of producers and writers on songs such as 'If It's Lovin' that You Want' and 'Let Me', and when *Music of the Sun* was released, it got rave reviews and stormed up the US album chart, reaching number 10. The first single, 'Pon de Replay', meanwhile, went to number one in New Zealand, number two in the US and UK, and made the top 10 in lots of other countries including Australia, Canada, Germany and Ireland. Wow!

There wasn't time for Rihanna to sit back and enjoy her success, however – she was far too busy! Just a month after *Music of the Sun* was released, she went to work on her second album, *A Girl Like Me*, and went on tour as the opening act for pop/rock star Gwen Stefani. Phew!

NEW INFLUENCES

Just eight months after her debut album was released, *A Girl Like Me* was launched. Jay-Z and her producers had encouraged Ri-Ri to listen to different types of music so she could experiment more on her second album. 'I was introduced to rock music,' she remembers, 'and that's now another one of my favourite types of music. I really enjoy listening to Fall Out Boy and Gwen Stefani.'

The first song she recorded for the new album was 'SOS', featuring a sample of the eighties song 'Tainted Love' by British band Soft Cell. 'I wasn't too familiar with Soft Cell, just because I'm 18 years old and I grew up in Barbados,' she said at the time – it's not surprising she'd never heard the song before as it was in the charts in 1981, seven years before Rihanna was born! The album also featured the song 'Unfaithful', written by Ne-Yo, 'We Ride', and 'Break It Off', which featured Jamaican artist Sean Paul (Rihanna had to fly to the lovely island of Jamaica to record the song with him – lucky girl!).

RIHANNA REVEALED

'I love making music. That's what I love to do… Every time we put out music, the whole process reflects whatever mood I'm in at that time. Whatever I'm feeling, whatever I'm going through, whatever mood I'm in… If I'm feeling like dancing or I'm feeling dark and vulnerable, then it will reflect in the music, too. So that's how we start.'

A GIRL LIKE ME

It was a very busy time as Rihanna was working on her new album while still doing interviews and promoting her first album! 'We were so busy promoting the first album while trying to get this one done, working some crazy hours,' she says. 'That's why this album, *A Girl Like Me*, is so close to me. I really put my heart and soul into it.'

Rihanna had performed some of the songs from *A Girl Like Me* when she had supported Gwen Stefani on tour, and she also appeared on MTV to promote the album's first single release, 'SOS'. All her hard work paid off – the single went to number one in the US, and reached the top five in Canada, Australia, New Zealand and the UK. Even better, the second single, 'Unfaithful', was another massive hit, reaching the top 10 in seven countries. Ri-Ri was on her way!

GOOD GIRL GONE BAD

At the beginning of her music career, Rihanna's management had wanted her to have a cute teen look – after all, she was only 17! But by the time she started recording her third album, *Good Girl Gone Bad*, she was 19 years old and ready for a tougher, more grown-up image – complete with a short, sharp haircut! 'We figured *Good Girl Gone Bad* was the perfect title because it showed people I'm my own person now,' she said at the time. 'Not doing what anyone wants me to do. I'm not the innocent Rihanna anymore. I'm taking a lot more risks and chances. I felt when I cut my hair, it shows people I'm not trying to look or be anybody else. The album is very edgy. We have some urban records, some really pop records.'

`UMBRELLA`

She also had some great collaborations, with Ne-Yo, Justin Timberlake and Timbaland – as well as recording a track with Def Jam president Jay-Z that was quite successful. It was, of course, 'Umbrella', a song that was originally written with Britney Spears in mind (bet she's mad she didn't record it now!). Released in March 2007, it rose up the charts around the world and won numerous awards including a Grammy for Rihanna and Jay-Z. In the UK it went straight to number one and stayed there for 10 weeks. If you hadn't heard of Rihanna before, by the summer of 2007, you certainly knew who she was!

The album featured three more big hits, 'Shut Up and Drive', 'Hate that I Love You' and 'Don't Stop the Music', and won Rihanna even more awards and great reviews. And if Ri-Ri wasn't doing enough already, she embarked on a worldwide tour to support the album that began in September 2007 and didn't end until January 2009! During the tour, Rihanna performed 80 shows throughout the US, Asia, Europe, Africa and Australia. And when she finished, there was no time to rest as there was another album to record!

'From the beginning, when we started making music, it was kind of always back to back — even with the second album that came, I would say, eight months after the first album was released, and then the third album came a year after that. So I've just never stopped making music. I love making music. That's what I love to do.'

RATED R

In 2008, Rihanna's life had often made the news, whether it was stories about her childhood in Barbados, or photos of her at premieres and award ceremonies rocking her new tough chick look. By November 2009, everyone was talking about her latest hit album, *Rated R*, an angrier, funkier album than her previous ones. 'It's definitely more edgy than the way we're used to seeing Rihanna. Let's call it "liberated,"' said Ne-Yo, who worked on tracks with the star. Justin Timberlake was full of praise, too. 'She broke onto the scene so hard with the last record and to have that many songs in the charts is impressive,' he said. 'I've heard some of the stuff on the record and it's awesome.'

The album was launched with a special concert in London that was broadcast online, and featured songs from the new album, including 'Russian Roulette', 'Hard' and 'Rude Boy'. By the end of the year, it had been voted the best pop album of the year. But far from sitting back and relaxing, Rihanna had another tour to do.

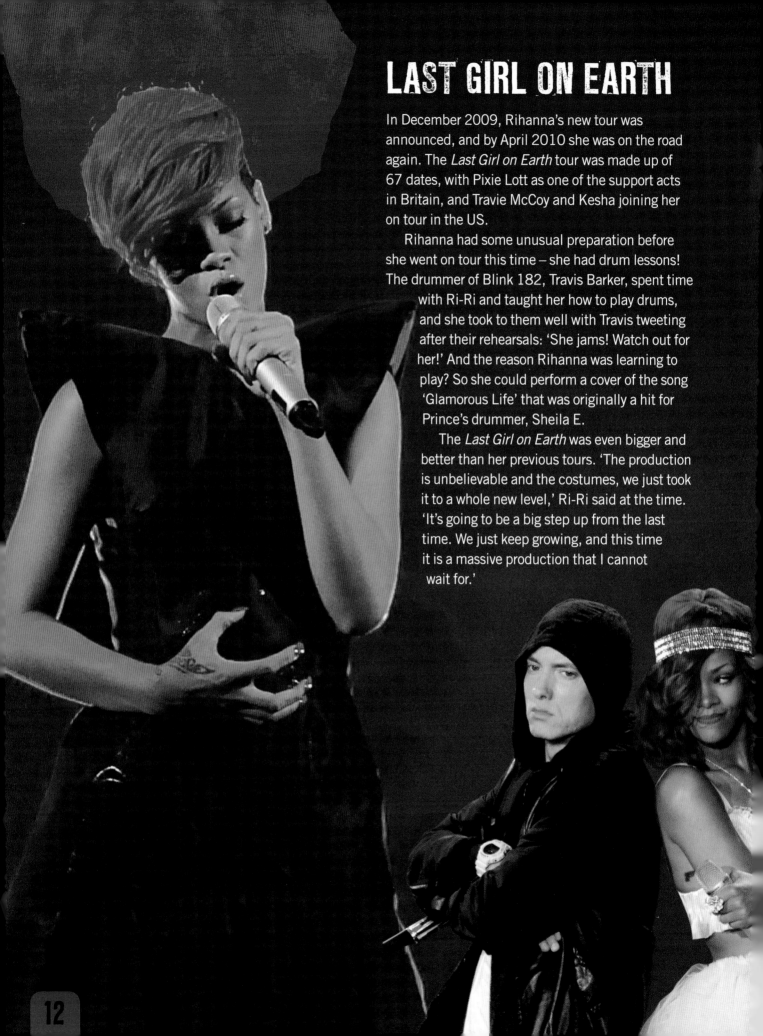

LAST GIRL ON EARTH

In December 2009, Rihanna's new tour was announced, and by April 2010 she was on the road again. The *Last Girl on Earth* tour was made up of 67 dates, with Pixie Lott as one of the support acts in Britain, and Travie McCoy and Kesha joining her on tour in the US.

Rihanna had some unusual preparation before she went on tour this time – she had drum lessons! The drummer of Blink 182, Travis Barker, spent time with Ri-Ri and taught her how to play drums, and she took to them well with Travis tweeting after their rehearsals: 'She jams! Watch out for her!' And the reason Rihanna was learning to play? So she could perform a cover of the song 'Glamorous Life' that was originally a hit for Prince's drummer, Sheila E.

The *Last Girl on Earth* was even bigger and better than her previous tours. 'The production is unbelievable and the costumes, we just took it to a whole new level,' Ri-Ri said at the time. 'It's going to be a big step up from the last time. We just keep growing, and this time it is a massive production that I cannot wait for.'

LOUD

When she wasn't rocking the stage, Rihanna was busy writing and recording another album, to be titled *Loud*, and working on a successful collaboration with Eminem that would become the hit single 'Love the Way You Lie' (also Rihanna's seventh number one in the US, and her first to sell a million copies in the UK). Without giving Rihanna time to catch her breath, *Loud* was released in November 2010, and featured the hits 'Only Girl (in the World)', 'What's My Name', 'S&M' and 'Man Down'. She followed it with the *Loud* tour in the summer of 2011, her longest so far with 98 dates, and managed to break a record by selling out 10 nights at London's O2 Arena, beating Britney Spears' previous record of eight, which had been the most sold out by a female artist.

TALK THAT TALK

Surely now it was time for Rihanna to have a rest? No! In October 2011, she teamed up with LA Reid as a guest mentor on the US version of the *X Factor*, helping him choose which male performers to mentor, and then she went back into the studio again to continue work on a new album, *Talk That Talk*.

The first single from *Talk That Talk* was 'We Found Love', featuring Calvin Harris, and it was another smash, featuring a video shot in a field in rural Ireland. Wearing a handkerchief style bikini top and jeans, Rihanna literally stopped traffic, as drivers strained to get a glimpse of her. Soon a crowd gathered, watching Rihanna sing along to the song, and lots of local school children filmed her on their phones. Lucky them!

The song went to number one in eight countries – including the UK and the USA – and she followed it with another hit, 'You Da One'. But as 2011 came to an end, Rihanna wasn't sure which song should be the album's third single. So on December 29th, she asked her fans on Twitter to vote for their favourite track. Four hours later, she had her answer and 'Talk That Talk' was released as a single in the US as 2012 began...

RIHANNA REVEALED

'There are people in the world who will love you and people in the world who will hurt you, and there are people in the world who will do both.'

It seems like Rihanna hasn't stopped working, recording and touring since her first hit in 2005, and 2012 was no different. Here are just some of the things that kept Ri-Ri busy during the year...

2012:
HIGHLIGHTS FROM RIHANNA'S YEAR...

TOURING

Rihanna kicked off the year by performing at the House of Blues in Hollywood, for a charity concert that also featured Calvin Harris, deadmau5 and Sebastian Ingrosso. The proceeds went to the Children's Orthopaedic Center and The Mark Taper-Johnny Mercer Artists Program at the Children's Hospital in Los Angeles.

She also played the Summer Sonic Festival in Japan in August 2012, alongside Green Day, Jamiroquai, Franz Ferdinand, Sigur Rós and New Order, and was the headline act at the free Hackney Weekend festival in June, one of more than 100 artists who played the stage over the weekend (Jay-Z, Florence + the Machine and Calvin Harris also performed).

Her biggest date of the year was at Hyde Park in London, where she was the headline act at the Wireless Festival on Sunday 8th July. Other performers on the day included Calvin Harris, Jessie J, the X Factor's Cher Lloyd and Kaskade.

RIHANNA REVEALED

'Never give up on your dreams. Keep holding onto them, and keep working to make it happen.'

AWARDS

Rihanna began the year on a high, as on 8th January, 2012, she was named the best-selling digital artist of all time in the US, having sold a massive 47,571,000 (yes, that's over 47 million!) singles and albums to date. Just three days later, on 11th January she won Favourite R&B Artist at the People's Choice Awards in LA.

At the Grammy Awards in LA on 12th February, Rihanna won two awards for her collaboration with Kanye West, 'All of the Lights'. They took home the awards for Best Rap Song and Best Rap/Sung Collaboration, meaning Rihanna has now won a total of six Grammys! And she still remembers winning her first one: 'When I won the first Grammy, there was no other feeling like that feeling. It just made me feel like I came so far, like that was just a dream a few years before that, and then it was happening right then. I went to the Grammies that year just to watch. I didn't even think we'd win.'

Rihanna amazed fans at the Brit Awards in February by performing 'We Found Love' in a glass box while dancers threw paint at the windows! Rihanna's efforts were rewarded as she won the Best Female International Artist Award for the second year in a row. She sent the following message to her fans after she won: 'Thanks to all my fans who continue to support me no matter what – I love you, this is for you. And at times when I feel misunderstood, my fans always remind me that it's okay to be myself and I will never forget you for that, so thank you.'

EVENTS

One of the main events to take up Rihanna's time in 2012 was the release of her first movie, *Battleship*. The excitement began with the world premiere in Tokyo on 3rd April, where Rihanna joined director Peter Berg and co-stars, Taylor Kitsch and Brooklyn Decker, in celebrating the movie's release with 5,000 screaming fans at the Yoyogi National Gymnasium in Japan.

RIHANNA REVEALED

'I always like something that's a little off, so it's just not typical or expected.' R

MUSIC

Following the release of her album *Talk That Talk* in November 2011, Rihanna not only released tracks from her own album as new singles, but in early 2012 she also released two collaborations with other artists: 'Princess of China' with Coldplay and 'Take Care' with Drake. She also performed on Chris Brown's single 'Turn Up the Music' in February 2012.

OTHER PROJECTS

In January 2012, it was announced that Rihanna would be working on a new TV show with Girls Aloud star Nicola Roberts to be shown on Sky Living TV in the summer. Nicola would present the show that was looking for undiscovered fashion talent, while Rihanna would work behind the scenes as Executive Producer as well as appearing on camera herself. The winner of the competition got to design an outfit for Rihanna to wear on stage.

Rihanna also launched her second perfume and called it 'Rebelle', which was her grandmother's nickname for her when she was a girl. 'My new fragrance is about taking control but still being a lady. There's a feminine, romantic element to the fragrance – but there's also a defiant quality in it,' she says.

RIHANNA REVEALED

'I think the role model thing is something that was definitely a lot more focused on, and there was all the pressure on it, in the first two years of my career, but I think what my fans enjoy about me are my flaws and my imperfections and the fact that I am rebellious and do things my way. I think it motivates them to be individuals, so that's all I care about – people being themselves and living that to the fullest.'

Since she rose to pop stardom in 2005, Rihanna has often talked about the music and musicians who have influenced her, and her sound. Here's her thoughts on the music stars that have made a difference to her own career...

BOB MARLEY

Ri-Ri loves the reggae star so much, she turned a room in her house into a shrine to him! 'The Bob Marley room is my loungey room, so there's incense burning, there's a painting on the wall of Bob Marley in black and white, which I love. The rest of the room goes from green into yellow into red, like the Jamaican flag,' she says. 'There's a little coffee table and these seats that are like big pillows on the floor, so it's not formal at all. There are lots of Bob Marley books, lyric books. He's one of my favourite artists of all time – he really paved the way for every other artist out of the Caribbean.'

GWEN STEFANI

Rihanna first met Gwen Stefani when she was asked to be the opening act for the rock singer's 2005 tour. 'Coming from Barbados, I really hadn't heard that much rock music,' Rihanna confesses. 'Touring with Gwen changed my perspective.' As well as performing with the band, Gwen is a fashion designer with her own label, L.A.M.B. (which stands for Love, Angel, Music, Baby), and she – like Rihanna – has also appeared in a movie, starring as legendary actress Jean Harlow in *The Aviator* in 2004.

BEYONCÉ

Ri-Ri is, of course, signed to Def Jam records, which is run by Beyoncé's husband Jay-Z, but the influence on Rihanna's career doesn't stop there. When Rihanna first became a star, she was often described as the 'Barbadian Beyoncé', and of course, she sang a Destiny's Child song when she first auditioned for Evan Rogers. Since then, the ladies' paths have often crossed, first when Rihanna's career was just beginning. 'I did an industry performance and Beyoncé came,' she remembers. 'I froze. I whispered, "You're my idol. Thank you for coming." And she said, "Ahh you're so cute!"'

MARIAH CAREY

With her phenomenal voice, Mariah has been compared to Aretha Franklin and Celine Dion, and she has scored hit after hit in her two decade career. In fact, when Rihanna's first single 'Pon de Replay' was released, it was held off the number one spot by Mariah's song, 'We Belong Together'! 'I looked up to Mariah a lot and I still do,' Rihanna said at the time. 'I admire her as an artist, and to compete with her to be at number one was a moment I will never forget for the rest of my life.'

MADONNA

The Queen of Pop is a huge influence on Ri-Ri. 'I think that Madonna was a great inspiration for me, especially on my earlier work. I had to examine her evolution through time; I think she reinvented her clothing style and music with success every single time. And at the same time remained a real force in entertainment in the whole world.'

JANET JACKSON

Michael Jackson's little sister is, of course, a star in her own right, and her combination of dancing and singing on stage was a big influence to Rihanna. 'She was one of the first female pop icons that I could relate to,' Rihanna has said. 'She was so vibrant and she had so much energy. She still has power. I've seen her on stage, and she can stand there for 20 minutes and have the whole arena scream at her. You have to love Janet.

RIHANNA`S HITS

Can you name every one of Rihanna`s hits? If so, you`re a superfan with an amazing memory, as she has recorded six albums and released over 40 singles!

Here's a list of all her amazing hits so you can make sure you have all of them in your collection. Score 5 points for each single you have, and 10 points for each album... if you score more than 200, you're one of Ri-Ri's most dedicated fans. Well done!

SINGLES

'Pon de Replay'

'If It's Lovin' that You Want'

'SOS'

'Unfaithful'

'We Ride'

'Break It Off' (featuring Sean Paul)

'Umbrella' (featuring Jay-Z)

'Shut Up and Drive'

'Hate that I Love You' (featuring Ne-Yo)

'Don't Stop the Music'

'Roll It' (J-Status featuring Shontelle and Rihanna)

'Take a Bow'

'Disturbia'

'Rehab'

'If I Never See Your Face Again' (Maroon 5 featuring Rihanna)

'Live Your Life' (T.I. featuring Rihanna)

'Russian Roulette'

'Hard' (featuring Jeezy)

'Run This Town' (Jay-Z featuring Rihanna and Kanye West)

'Rude Boy'

'Rockstar 101' (featuring Slash)

'Te Amo'

'Only Girl (In The World)'

'What's My Name?' (featuring Drake)

'Raining Men' (featuring Nicki Minaj)

'S&M'

'California King Bed'

'Man Down'

'Love the Way You Lie' (Eminem featuring Rihanna)

'Who's that Chick?' (David Guetta featuring Rihanna)

'Cheers' (Drink To That)

'We Found Love' (featuring Calvin Harris)

'You Da One'

'All of the Lights' (Kanye West featuring Rihanna and Kid Cudi)

'Fly' (Nicki Minaj featuring Rihanna)

'Talk That Talk' (featuring Jay-Z)

'Birthday Cake' (featuring Chris Brown)

'Princess of China' (Coldplay featuring Rihanna)

'Take Care' (Drake featuring Rihanna)

ALBUMS

Music of the Sun (released August 2005)

A Girl Like Me (released April 2006)

Good Girl Gone Bad (released May 2007)

Rated R (released November 2009)

Loud (released November 2010)

Talk That Talk (released November 2011)

So how many do you have? Think you've got them all? Well, don't forget Rihanna has also appeared on some charity songs, too! There's 'Just Stand Up!', part of the Stand Up to Cancer campaign, 'Redemption Song', released to raise money after the 2010 Haiti earthquake, and also 'Stranded (Haiti Mon Amour)', which she sang with Bono, Jay-Z and The Edge, which was on the 2010 Haiti earthquake album *Hope For Haiti Now*.

How much do you know about Rihanna? Here`s a quick recap on all things Ri-Ri for you to test just how much you know about the star. Find out on the opposite page if you can earn the title of the world`s biggest fan... or if you need to brush up on your knowledge!

NO.1 FAN QUIZ

1. What music is Rihanna 'super influenced' by?
a. Reggae music
b. Musicals
c. Country music

2. What song did Ri-Ri sing at her first meeting with music execs?
a. 'Emotion' by Destiny's Child
b. 'Hero' by Mariah Carey
c. 'Single Ladies' by Beyoncé

3. What was the name of Rihanna's debut album?
a. Music in the Sun
b. Music of the Sun
c. Music about the Sun

4. What is the name of the song that was a a huge, global success?
a. 'Raincoat'
b. 'Umbrella'
c. 'Wellies'

5. Which pop princess became Rihanna's BFF as she rose to fame?
a. Britney Spears
b. Christina Aguilera
c. Katy Perry

6. Which reality US TV show was Rihanna a mentor for?
a. The Voice
b. American Idol
c. X Factor

7. What is the name of Ri-Ri's own perfume?
a. Rihanna
b. Rebelle
c. Rock Star

8. Where is Rihanna from?
a. Boston
b. Bermuda
c. Barbados

1. A- REGGAE MUSIC
2. A -'EMOTION' BY DESTINY'S CHILD
3. B - MUSIC OF THE SUN
4. B - 'UMBRELLA'
5. C - KATY PERRY
6. C - X FACTOR
7. B - REBELLE
8. C - BARBADOS

SCORES:

IF YOU SCORED 0 - 3:
Better luck next time – it was a very tough quiz.

IF YOU SCORED 4 - 7:
Well done. Perhaps another swotting session ais needed and you'll score even higher next time!

IF YOU SCORED 8 - 10:
Congratulations! You probably know Ri-Ri's songs better than she does! A true fan indeed!

Invite your friends to a Rihanna-themed sleepover! Pick your favourite songs from her albums to make a party music playlist, and decorate your bedroom with some Rihanna posters. And what should you eat? Rihanna cupcakes, of course!

HAVE A RIHANNA SLEEPOVER!

TO DECORATE YOUR ROOM FOR A PARTY SLEEPOVER YOU
WILL NEED:

+ Large pictures of Rihanna taken from magazines

+ Coloured paper

+ Scissors

+ Glue

+ Lots of different coloured glitters or gold and
  silver confetti

1. Carefully cut out large pictures you like of Rihanna from magazines using the scissors.

2. Take a piece of coloured paper that is larger than the photo you are using. Glue the photo to the paper, so you have a border of coloured paper around the picture of Rihanna, like a frame.

3. Put a little glue on the coloured paper (you can make patterns if you like, just glue the corners, or glue all around the Rihanna photo) and then sprinkle glitter or confetti on the glue.

4. Allow to dry. You now have a pretty, sparkly poster of Rihanna to put on the wall for your party!

Alternatively, if you have a very big sheet of coloured paper, you could glue lots of smaller pictures of Rihanna to it, and then decorate it with glitter to make one big Rihanna poster!

HOW TO MAKE RIHANNA CUPCAKES!

YOU WILL NEED:

+ 250g (8oz) unsalted butter, softened (just get it out of the fridge an hour before you need it)

+ 250g (8oz) caster sugar

+ 250g (8oz) self-raising flour

+ Pinch of salt

+ 4 medium eggs

+ 4 tablespoons milk

+ 24 paper cases

+ 2 x 12-hole muffin tins

+ For the buttercream icing:

+ 220g butter, softened

+ 1kg icing sugar

+ 2 tsp vanilla extract

+ 120ml milk

+ Icing decorations such as iced flowers, edible glitter or chocolate sprinkles (optional)

1. Turn the oven on to 190ºC/Gas Mark 5 – it may be a good idea to get an adult to help you.

2. Put the butter in a large bowl and beat it (or use an electric whisk) until soft and creamy.

3. Add the sugar, flour, salt, eggs and milk and whisk until it's smooth with no lumpy bits.

4. Using a spoon, divide the mixture between all the 24 paper cases that you have put in the muffin tins.

5. Place the muffin tins in the oven and bake for 15 minutes. Swap the tins around and bake for another few minutes so all the cakes turn golden.

6. To check the cakes are cooked, take one tin out of the oven and place a skewer or cocktail stick in the centre of one of the cakes. If it comes out clean with no uncooked mixture on it, the cakes are cooked!

7. Take the tins out of the oven and remove the cupcakes from the tins, and leave to cool on a wire rack.

8. When the cakes are cooled from the oven it's time to ice them! Put the butter, icing sugar and vanilla extract in a large mixing bowl and beat with an electric whisk for about 5 minutes until the mixture is smooth.

9. Using a teaspoon, scoop some of the icing out of the bowl and place on a cake. Now take a knife and spread it as evenly as you can. Decorate each cake in this way and then keep in a cool place until you're ready to party!

drowning, as well as train with real naval officers to understand the part she was playing. 'We worked with real military people, you know, people in the Navy, people who have fought in Iraq before,' she told the UGO website in an interview. 'This one man, Donald, he pretty much drilled me, yelled at me, made me do push-ups. Everything. It really got you in the mentality, that's the things they really go through, you know, when they first sign up. It's not a walk in the park.'

Her role was just as tough as the men's roles, as she told Capital FM: 'my character is a Weapons Officer; she's tattooed up and she's in control of the weapons on the ship. She knows everything about every single weapon – it's a really cool role. It's really surreal to be in the centre of all that for my first film, but I'm really comfortable working in that group.'

Her co-stars included *John Carter* star Taylor Kitsch, *True Blood's* Alexander Skarsgard (lucky Ri-Ri!) and Liam Neeson, three macho men who play US naval officers based at Pearl Harbor who have to battle against an alien species to save the world. In an interview, Taylor reported Rihanna did her own stunts and was 'annihilating everything in her way', so she certainly held her own alongside her male co-stars!

RIHANNA QUIZ

**How well do you know Rihanna?
Try our quick quiz and find out...**

1) IS RIHANNA'S FAVOURITE SONG:

+ 'Vision of Love' by Mariah Carey

+ 'Teenage Dream' by Katy Perry

+ 'Thriller' by Michael Jackson

+ 'Holiday' by Madonna

2) WHAT IS RIHANNA'S FAVOURITE TYPE OF HOLIDAY?

+ Camping in a field in England

+ Skiing during the day and staying in a mountainside chalet at night

+ Relaxing by the ocean and staying in a secluded villa

+ An activity weekend at Center Parcs

3) WHAT IS RIHANNA'S FAVOURITE TV SHOW?

+ Eastenders

+ Spongebob Squarepants

+ CSI

+ Entourage

4) WHAT IS RIHANNA'S REAL FIRST NAME?

+ Robin

+ Rorrey

+ Robyn

+ Rajad

5) RIHANNA DUETTED WITH A FAMOUS MUSIC ARTIST ON THE SONG 'LOVE THE WAY YOU LIE'. WHO WAS IT?

+ Katy Perry

+ Eminem

+ Britney Spears

+ Chris Brown

6) 'I THINK SHE IS THE MOST
BEAUTIFUL WOMAN I HAVE EVER SEEN.
LIKE, HOW DO YOU HAVE A FACE LIKE
THAT, WITH HAIR LIKE THAT AND
DIMPLES, AND A BODY LIKE THAT,
THAT'S PROPORTIONED LIKE THAT?'
WHO IS RIHANNA TALKING ABOUT?

+ Britney Spears

+ Katy Perry

+ Cheryl Cole

+ Scarlett Johansson

7) WHICH TROPICAL ISLAND IS
RIHANNA FROM?

+ Barbados

+ The Bahamas

+ Jamaica

+ St Lucia

8) WAS RIHANNA'S 2009 ALBUM
CALLED:

+ *Rated PG*

+ *Rated R*

+ *Rated U*

+ *Rated 15*

9) WHAT WAS THE 'RIHANNA
CURSE' OF 2007?

+ All her singles that year went
to number two but never made it
to number one.

+ Every time she sung 'Umbrella'
on stage, one of her backing
dancers fell over.

+ The Sun newspaper spotted
that it rained for nine weeks
somewhere in Britain from the
moment 'Umbrella' went to number
one that summer.

+ She lost her voice for three
months just as Umbrella went
to number one.

10) WHICH OF THESE ARTISTS DID NOT
RECORD OR PERFORM A VERSION OF
RIHANNA'S HIT SONG 'UMBRELLA'?

+ Jamie Cullum

+ McFly

+ JLS

+ Susan Boyle

Anwers on page 62

BEST FRIENDS AND FIRST LOVES: A GUIDE TO THE PEOPLE IN RIHANNA'S LIFE

She may be constantly in the recording studio or on tour, but Rihanna always finds time for the important people in her life – her brothers, her parents, and, of course, her friends. Check out the special people in Ri-Ri's life...

KATY PERRY

One of Ri-Ri's best friends is also her music rival, Katy Perry. The 27-year-old 'Firework' singer from California and Rihanna are often up for the same awards, but they have become great friends anyway! The gal pals often tweet about each other, have been on holiday together, and plan to work together on a single, too. 'She is one of my favourite musicians as well as one of my favourite people in the industry,' Rihanna says of Katy. 'She's very uncalculated, very sure of herself, and that's something that's very rare in this industry to find. We connected really quickly.'

'Honestly, I really love Katy... When I met her, it was such a breath of fresh air. I just couldn't believe this chick had no edit button. She was everything I wanted to be at that time, because I was still at a point in my career where I had to edit myself and not be too open.'

RIHANNA REVEALED

JAY-Z

Rihanna is, of course, signed to Jay-Z's Def Jam record label, and he was one of the first people to hear her sing and know she was going to be a star! Since then, Jay-Z has helped Rihanna through all stages of her career, advising her on how to deal with fame and, of course, lending his voice to some of her songs including the smash hit 'Umbrella'. And, back in the early days of her career, he even talked to potential boyfriends before they asked Rihanna out! 'He's very protective. Jay has my best interests in mind.'

MELISSA FORDE

Ri-Ri's personal assistant Melissa is also her best friend, and the pop star often turns to her for advice, as she told *Cosmopolitan* magazine: 'Melissa always says to me, "You need to let your guard down." Because even if a guy texts me or says something and he's trying to be slick, I would never entertain it. I think it's just an act.' 26-year-old Melissa, who grew up in the same part of Barbados as Rihanna, often tweets pictures of Rihanna while they are out together, and Ri-Ri has been known to take pics of her BFF and tweet them to her followers, too!

KANYE WEST

Rapper, singer and record producer Kanye West is a fan and a friend of Rihanna's. 'Rihanna has the potential to be, you know, the greatest artist of all time and, in that sense, I feel like she is my baby sis,' Kanye said in an interview in 2009. The pair have worked together on and off since Rihanna became a star: she toured with Kanye in 2008, and also appeared in the video for his single 'Paranoid' in 2009. They worked together again on the single 'Run This Town' with Jay-Z. Their latest collaboration is the song 'All of the Lights', which won two Grammy Awards in 2012.

MATT KEMP

Matt Kemp is a baseball player for the Los Angeles Dodgers, and he and Rihanna dated in 2010, and at the time she described their relationship as 'so easy'. 'I have such a chaotic life, but at the end of the day, that is just my peace,' she said in June of that year. 'It keeps me sane, really, talking to him and talking to my family.' The pair met through friends in November 2009, and were spotted on holiday together in Mexico two months later. Unfortunately they split at the end of 2010, but remain friends.

RIHANNA WORDSEARCH

Can you find all ten words in the grid? Words may be written forwards, backwards or diagonally.

R a n
R D a h
A
N
O L
A
34

R	R	G	E	S	A	P	U	M	B	R	E	L	L	A
N	F	I	T	Y	L	P	O	Z	U	A	S	H	O	P
U	R	M	R	A	T	E	D	R	S	B	V	U	X	O
S	R	T	I	I	R	E	U	O	L	T	A	P	R	N
E	I	I	H	J	K	P	S	A	C	A	P	Q	C	D
H	J	P	A	Z	L	D	O	T	W	X	O	B	D	E
T	X	R	N	A	P	F	W	A	Y	H	A	A	K	R
F	A	I	N	K	L	L	T	E	A	T	S	R	A	E
O	W	H	A	W	O	Z	O	U	T	D	N	B	D	P
C	J	I	N	R	B	V	M	L	O	U	D	A	W	L
I	F	T	B	A	I	N	E	N	S	T	M	D	V	A
S	R	S	O	V	A	S	F	E	T	L	Q	O	S	Y
U	I	R	I	O	H	I	R	C	O	O	U	S	E	R
M	Z	S	T	I	L	C	O	P	U	H	R	O	N	A
H	A	C	P	L	L	H	J	A	Y	Z	J	L	T	Z

+ Rihanna

+ Loud

+ Rated R

+ Umbrella

+ Jay-Z

+ Ri-Ri

+ Battleship

+ 'Pon de Replay'

+ Music of the Sun

+ Barbados

DO NOT DISTURB!

YOU WILL NEED:

+ A piece of cardboard (part of a cereal box would work well)

+ Scissors

+ Glue

+ Coloured pens

+ Glitter pens or glitter glue

+ Two different pictures of Rihanna cut from magazines – perhaps one of her smiling and one of her striking a moody pose!

INSTRUCTIONS:

1. Draw a door-hanger shape (or copy the one below) onto the piece of card.

2. Cut out the card carefully with scissors.

3. Take the smiling picture of Rihanna and, using the glue, stick it to one side of the card. Don't forget to leave some space so you can write 'It's great to see you, come on in!' above the picture.

4. Stick the more serious photo on the other side of the card and leave enough space to write 'Do Not Disturb! I'm busy doing my hair!'

5. Use coloured pens and glitter pens to give the hook of the door hanger some sparkle, or add some stickers to cover up the last bits of card that show through.

6. You're finished! Once the glue is all dry, you can hang your Rihanna door hanger on your door!

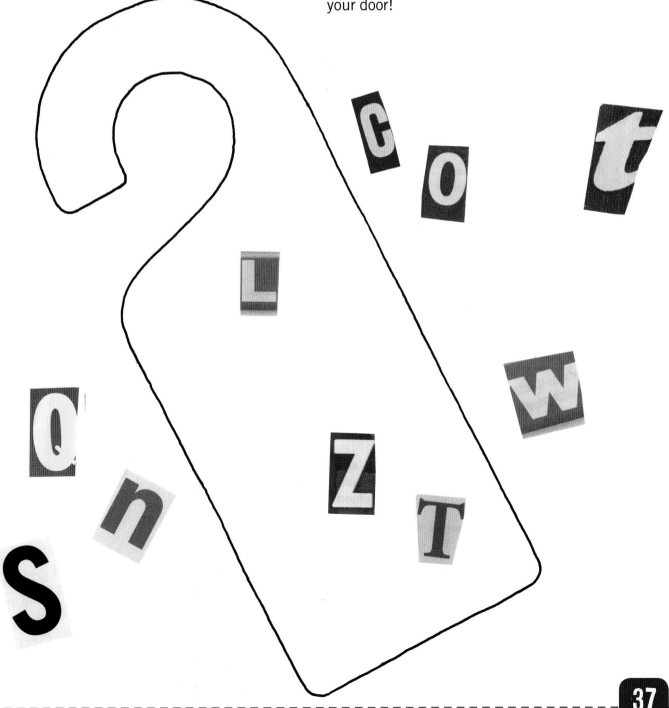

Whether she`s on stage, on TV or just off to the shops, Rihanna always looks fashionable and funky, and is known for her unique sense of style. But could you dress Rihanna better than she dresses herself? Here`s your chance to style a star using the mannequins over the next few pages...

STYLIST FOR A DAY!

You will need:

+ Coloured pens

+ Glue

+ Scissors

+ Glitter or glitter glue

+ Sheets of coloured paper (or white paper to colour on)

WHAT TO DO:

1. Using coloured paper, cut out clothes shapes using the outlines on the next few pages. (If you've got some tracing or greaseproof paper around the house, you can copy the outlines then trace them onto coloured paper and then cut the shapes out).

2. Colour in and decorate the clothes any way you wish! You can add glitter, sparkles, flowery designs – whatever you like.

3. Using the glue, stick your new outfit to the different Rihanna mannequins and she's ready to go out and have fun!

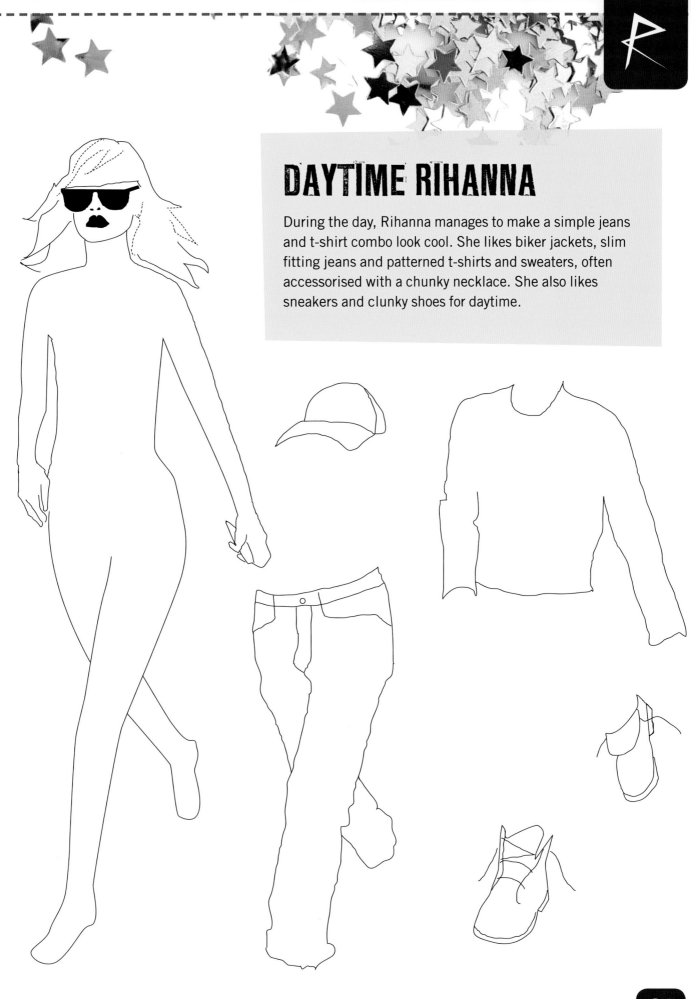

DAYTIME RIHANNA

During the day, Rihanna manages to make a simple jeans and t-shirt combo look cool. She likes biker jackets, slim fitting jeans and patterned t-shirts and sweaters, often accessorised with a chunky necklace. She also likes sneakers and clunky shoes for daytime.

ROCKIN` RIHANNA

On stage, Rihanna's outfits have often been described as risqué, as they often feature corsets, tiny dresses, and bikini tops. They're also bright and colourful – she's worn a shiny neon blue coat, a luminous yellow dress and another made of gold circles on stage, so even the audience at the back can see her! So let your imagination go wild designing an eye-catching outfit for her to wear in front of her fans!

RIHANNA ON THE TOWN

For premieres, nights on the town and awards ceremonies, Rihanna does like her designer labels, from Dolce & Gabbana to Herve Leger to Armani. She'll often wear a bodycon dress to an important night out, complete with sky-high heels or ankle boots, but occasionally she'll surprise with a full-on evening dress, though always one that's more edgy than traditional.

RIHANNA
TRUE OR
FALSE?

Here are some statements about
Rihanna`s life. But are they true
or false? See how many you get
right and find out how devoted
a fan you are!

1. Rihanna's first movie appearance is in the 2012 movie *Battleship*.

2. When she auditioned for Evan Rogers, she sang Destiny's Child's version of 'Emotion'.

3. Rihanna's first hit was 'Pon de Replay'.

4. Rihanna's hair is insured for $5 million.

5. There is a Rihanna wax figure at Madame Tussaud's Wax Museum in London.

6. Rihanna has designed clothes for Versace.

7. Rihanna calls her fans the 'Rihanna Navy'.

8. She has red hair on the cover of her album *Loud*.

9. The song 'SOS' features a sample of the eighties track 'Tainted Love'. The original version of the song was recorded by Duran Duran.

10. The video for Rihanna's duet with Eminem, 'Love the Way You Lie', features Transformers actress Megan Fox and Lost star Dominic Monaghan as fighting lovers.

11. Eminem recorded 'Love the Way You Lie' together with Rihanna in a recording studio in London.

12. Coldplay have sung their own version of Rihanna's 'We Found Love'.

13. Rihanna's sixth album is called *Walk That Walk*.

14. Rihanna banned umbrellas at her UK concerts.

15. There is a national holiday in Barbados to honour Rihanna.

16. Beyoncé runs Def Jam, Rihanna's record label.

17. Rihanna's co-star in *Battleship* is Liam Neeson. He has played a lion in a movie.

18. Rihanna appeared in the movie *Bring It On: All Or Nothing*. One of the lead roles was played by Beyoncé.

19. Her favourite subject at school was P.E.

20. Rihanna has a pet – a Pomeranian dog named Marley.

Answers on page 62

So what's it like being on tour with Rihanna? Come join her band and all will be revealed.

RIHANNA: BACKSTAGE PASS

VIP PASS

HER DRESSING ROOM

During her *Last Girl on Earth* tour in 2010, Rihanna had a tour 'rider' that listed all the things she needed in her dressing room on each night of the tour. This included:

+ A dressing room that could hold at least 6 people, with a clean shower and toilet

+ Relaxed lighting (lamps rather than overhead strip lighting)

+ Drapes (white chiffon) over any lockers or bare walls (many of her tour dates were in stadiums more frequently used by football teams so her dressing room would often be a converted locker room) and carpet on the floor

+ A full-length mirror

+ A 6ft comfortable couch/sofa in white, but not leather

+ Throw pillows in cheetah or leopard print – no sequins

+ A large rug in animal print

+ Archipelago Black Forest scented candles

+ A square vase of white tulips or lilies

HER CREW

Rihanna's stage tours often include fireworks, fantastic light shows and amazing things happening on stage – she's had a life-size pink army tank to dance around – so quite a lot of people are needed on tour to make it all happen. As well as her management team, Rihanna's crew includes:

+ 5 directors who work on the staging and show direction

+ 5 choreographers, including one trained in aerial stunts

+ 1 martial arts consultant

+ At least 6 dancers

+ 5 stylists for hair, make up and clothes

+ Rihanna's band, including 3 guitarists, a drummer and 2 keyboard players

+ 2 backup singers

+ At least 15 production crew, including thetour manager, road manager, carpenters and technicians

+ A team of 6 caterers for all the backstage food

RIHANNA REVEALED

'My favourite food right now is microwave butter popcorn. And when I'm in London I'm close to authentic Jamaican food, so I tend to eat that every day.'

HER OUTFITS

During the *Good Girl Gone Bad* tour, Rihanna often took to the stage wearing leather shorts and bikini tops, while on the *Last Girl On Earth* tour she could be seen in bikini bottoms or shorts with wild jackets that often had extreme shoulders – one even had spikes coming out of it! For 2011's *Loud* Tour, Rihanna's outfits often looked futuristic, like a neon blue jacket she wore when performing in Ireland. She also wore hot pants and a bikini top for some numbers, a pair of shocking pink ankle boots and a jewel-encrusted bikini.

RIHANNA REVEALED

'We come up with different ideas and cool things that we can do on stage. Things that we've never seen before, daring things – then we start with the rehearsal and we get into the nitty-gritty and the details of everything. I love taking risks. I'm not afraid of the unknown.'

HER FANS

Rihanna calls her fans the Rihanna Navy, and there are always thousands – some of whom dress like her and dye their hair the same colour – on her tour. Near the end of the *Loud* tour, she tweeted how much she was going to miss her fans now the tour was over. 'Just 4 shows left before the #LOUDtour comes to an end! Can't believe we're here already! As much as i miss home, im gonna miss u guys.'

RIHANNA CROSSWORD

ACROSS

1. Who is Rihanna's mentor and owner of Def Jam records?

2. What is the name of Rihanna's first ever single?

3. Where was Rihanna born?

4. Who is Rihanna's pop star BFF?

DOWN

1. Which Queen of Pop was a big inspiration for Rihanna growing up?

2. What is the name of the album that Rihanna released in 2009?

3. 'Rihanna' is actually her middle name! So what is her real first name?

4. What is Rihanna's nickname?

5. Finish the name of Rihanna's album: Last Girl on _____

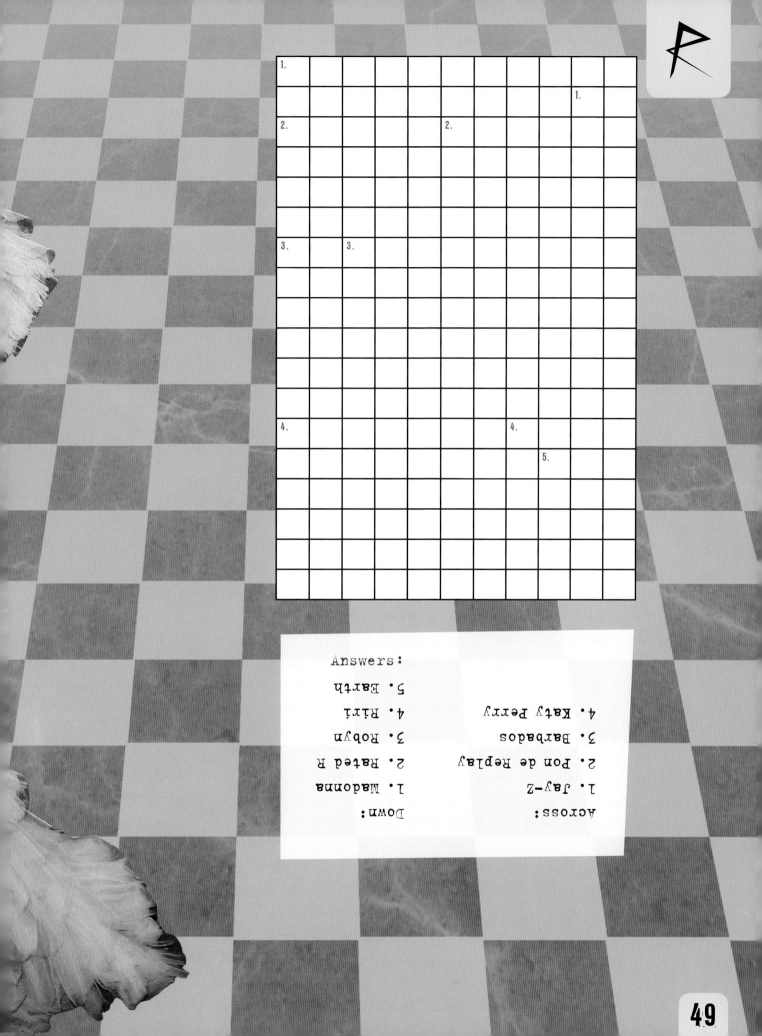

Answers:

Down:

1. Madonna
2. Rated R
3. Robyn
4. Riri
5. Earth

Across:

1. Jay-Z
2. Pon de Replay
3. Barbados
4. Katy Perry

RIHANNA'S HAIRSTYLES!

Rihanna's hair is naturally dark brown, and when she first started on the road to stardom, she wore it long and wavy. But in the last seven years, she has tried every length, every style and every colour you can possibly imagine! Below are some of her looks – why not cut out a picture of yourself and see which one suits you best!

BLONDE AND CURLY

TOP TIP: To get lots of ringlet-style curls like Ri-Ri, let your hair dry naturally after washing. Spritz a little curl styling spray on your hair and then take small sections of hair and curl lengthways using a curling brush or, better still, a curling iron. Hold the curl for a few seconds and then release. Repeat all over your head and allow the set curls to cool down. Once your hair is completely cool, shake your head to allow the curls to loosen (or, if really curly, run your fingers through your hair) and you're done!

BRIGHT RED AND WAVY

TOP TIP: For luxuriant waves, use a volumising styling product on wet hair, then slowly blow-dry your hair with a large brush, curling the ends towards your neck. You can add an extra touch by pinning a couple of sections of hair in rolls at the top of your head for extra height and style!

RED AND CRIMPED

TOP TIP: For wild, crimped hair like Rihanna's, you will need quite long, thick hair to start with. Wash and then blow-dry your hair upside down so it's as full as possible. Take small sections of hair and crimp, starting from the neckline and working up towards the top of your head. Allow to cool before you toss your head and spray with hairspray to keep the style.

A SLEEK BOB

TOP TIP: Perfect for shoulder-length hair. Simply wash and use a straightening styling product on your hair. Then blow-dry your hair in sections using a large round brush, curling into your face. Choose a side parting, and blow the last section of hair away from your face – that way you'll still be able to see where you're going!

SHORT, SHARP AND BLACK

TOP TIP: Rihanna has often had very short hair, sometimes with a shaved side and a long fringe and top section, so this is a style for the very brave. You would need a qualified hairdresser to cut and shave your hair, and then you just blow dry the longer parts into the style you want! Ri-Ri has had a bouffant quiff, a feathered fringe, top curls and even spiky hair with this style.

RIHANNA REVEALED

'We are always changing it up, experimenting, and having fun with hair,' Ri-Ri's stylist Ursula Stephen reveals. 'Her hairstyle typically changes depending on what's on our agenda, what she's wearing, or how she's feeling. We take it day by day and event by event.'

STEAL HER STYLE

Rihanna's style is all her own — she's gone from cute girl next door to one of the most stylish women in the world in just a few years. Everyone wants to look like her — so much so that when she appeared on Jonathon Ross's TV show in March 2012, the outfit she wore sold out the next day! Here are some of her most stylish moments...

IN THE BEGINNING

When Rihanna first moved to the US from Barbados to begin her music career, she dressed like a typical teenager: high street jeans, cropped t-shirts, trainers and big hoop earrings, and she wore her hair long. How things have changed since then! 'When I was fourteen and first started going out, I always wanted to be the opposite of everyone else. So I would go to the club in a polo T-shirt and pants and sneakers and a hat on backward, just so I would not be dressed like other girls. I got desperate for things that weren't available in Barbados.'

DAYTIME

Ri-Ri still wears jeans, but now they're J Brand or Armani (whom she has advertised for) and she teams them with ankle boots or high heels rather than sneakers. If the weather's warm enough, out come the shorts and teeny tops! 'Getting dressed, I want to pick the most bizarre pair of shorts so I can figure out how to make it look right, or work an outfit that will make people go, "What is she wearing?!"'

ONSTAGE

Rihanna's on-stage style is a little raunchier than what she wears the rest of the time! She wears little leather bikinis, hot pants covered in jewels, and thigh high boots. 'It's always fun to take some of the outfits home. Sometimes I get to do that. I like to push the envelope sometimes, when it comes to what I wear onstage.'

GOING OUT

With her amazing figure, Rihanna looks great in everything, and she shows it in body-con dresses by Herve Leger, flowing cutaway gowns by Gucci, a lace dress by Stella McCartney or something ruffly by Jean-Paul Gaultier. 'The thrill in fashion for me is taking a risk and daring myself to make it work. Even when I go shopping, I always buy something twisted and I know I'm going to have to figure out somehow to pull it off and make it my own.'

ON TV

Did you fall in love with that stunning red dress Rihanna wore on the cover of her single 'Only Girl (In the World)'? Start saving – the dress was by Marchesa and was worth about £5,000! 'I'm a big fan of mini-dresses – they're my favorite silhouette – because they're flirty and you get to show a little skin without revealing too much, especially if the sleeves are long and cover up a lot of the body. I also like dresses that come to the knee that are a little tight and show off the shape of the body.'

HER INSPIRATION

Rihanna is a huge fan of Kate Moss and her style. 'I really admire Kate because every photo shoot she does is different. Every time you see her there is a different energy that she puts out in whatever outfit she is wearing. I think she is amazing.'

THE NEXT VICTORIA BECKHAM?

She's already designed T-shirts and accessories for Armani, and in March 2012 Rihanna revealed that she'd like to work more in fashion as time goes by. 'I want to design. I want to earn it… So I'm working with designers that I respect, and fashion companies that I respect. I want people to really trust me before I just say "buy it because it's mine."'

RIHANNA`S HOROSCOPE

Rihanna was born on 20 February 1988, which makes her a Pisces. Pisceans are often gifted in the creative arts, especially art and music – no surprise, then, that Rihanna has become a successful singing star! They are sometimes a bit gossipy and not the best at keeping secrets. Pisceans love quiet and beautiful places so Rihanna was extra lucky to grow up in the pretty and peaceful surroundings of Barbados.

Pisceans are kind, caring and thoughtful, but they can become tough and be in charge if they need to – they are hard working and dedicated to achieving their goals. That certainly sounds like a very famous pop singer that we know!

Other famous Pisceans include:

+ Bruce Willis

+ Charlotte Church

+ Drew Barrymore

+ Eva Mendes

THE YEAR AHEAD FOR RIHANNA

The next year is going to be a busy one for Pisceans like Rihanna. People will recognise her talents and abilities in fields other than music and the offers of work will flood in — perhaps another movie role following her performance in Battleship?

She'll still have time for her music, of course, and over the year there is much prosperity predicted for Pisceans, possibly meaning Rihanna will have another number one hit or album.

On the personal side, Pisceans are known to be dreamy and romantic, and love could be in the air for Rihanna over the next 365 days. But who will be the lucky boy? Pisceans get on well with those born under the following signs: Cancer, Scorpio, Taurus and Gemini.

Finally, Pisceans are often good at many things. As well as music and acting, Rihanna has expressed an interest in fashion design and she has already launched her own perfumes. Could the next year see her become a fashion designer? Wait and see...

'My fans aren't followers. We're peers. They're right here with me. I need them more than they need me. I need their feedback, I need their honesty, and I need their support. Without that, it's pointless.'

RIHANNA – THE FUTURE

So what's next for Rihanna? In an interview with Jonathon Ross in March 2012, she hinted that a career in movies might be her next move... but throughout the year she also told interviewers she'd like to be a fashion designer too!

Certainly, she's multi-talented enough to do both and maintain her pop idol status, too. At just 24 years of age, there is plenty of time for her to become a movie star, clothes designer and continue her reign as pop queen. We'll have to wait and see... Whatever Ri-Ri does next, we're sure it'll be breathtaking!

PICTURE CREDITS

Courtesy of Getty Images

ACKNOWLEDGEMENTS

Posy Edwards would like to Jo Berry, Jane Sturrock, Nicola Crossley, Helen Ewing and Smith & Gilmour.

Copyright © Orion 2012

First published in hardback in Great Britain in 2012 by Orion Books an imprint of the Orion Publishing Group Ltd, Orion House, 5 Upper St Martin's Lane, London WC2H 9EA

An Hachette UK Company

10 9 8 7 6 5 4 3 2 1

A CIP catalogue record for this book is available from the British Library.

ISBN: 978 4091 0943 3

Designed by Smith & Gilmour

Printed and bound in Germany by Mohn Media

The Orion Publishing Group's policy is to use papers that are natural, renewable and recyclable and made from wood grown in sustainable forests. The logging and manufacturing processes are expected to conform to the environmental regulations of the country of origin.

Every effort has been made to fulfil requirements with regard to reproducing copyright material. The author and publisher will be glad to rectify any omissions at the earliest opportunity.

www.orionbooks.co.uk

ANSWERS

Rihanna Quiz

1 – a   2 – c   3 – d   4 – c   5 – b
6 – c   7 – a   8 – b   9 – c   10 – d

Rihanna Wordsearch

	R					U	M	B	R	E	L	L	A
N		I											P
U			R	A	T	E	D	R					O
S			I	I									N
E			H										D
H			A								B		E
T			N							A	A		R
F			N						T		R		E
O			A					T			B		P
C							L	O	U	D	A		L
I						E					D		A
S						S					O		Y
U				H							S		
M			I										
			P			J	A	Y	Z				

Rihanna: True of False?

1 False 2 True 3 True   4 False 5 True
6 False 7 True 8 True   9 False 10 True
11 False 12 True 13 False 14 True 15 True
16 False 17 True 18 False 19 False 20 True

Rihanna Crossword

J	A	Y	Z							
									M	
P	O	N	D	E	R	E	P	L	A	Y
					A				D	
					T				O	
					E				N	
B	A	R	B	A	D	O	S		N	
		O			R				A	
		B								
		Y								
		N								
K	A	T	Y	P	E	R	R	Y		
							I	E		
							R	A		
							I	R		
							T			
							H			